SLA GUIDELI

CW00392363

Everything in its Place

Managing Electronic and
Physical Resources in the
School Library

Kathy Lemaire and
Sally Duncan

Series Editor: Geoff Dubber

Acknowledgements

This Guideline has updated the SLA Guideline *Shelf Life, Shelf Matters* published in 2004. All text and figures have been thoroughly revised and updated. We are grateful to IS Oxford, MLS and Softlink for supplying screenshots of their library management systems.

Published by

School Library Association
1 Pine Court, Kembrey Park
Swindon
SN2 8AD

Tel: 01793 530166   Fax: 01793 481182
E-mail: info@sla.org.uk
Web: www.sla.org.uk

Registered Charity No: 313660
Charity Registered in Scotland No: SC039453

Cover photographs by Philip Cooper Photography
Printed by Holywell Press, Oxford

Contents

Introduction

Libraries have always been seen as essential to education, both formal and self-directed. In our information rich society they are even more important as the place to go to obtain information in all its forms, whether in books or e-books, in archives or on the Internet. They are even more important as the place to go to find advice and guidance on making sense of all the information available. Effective school libraries, or learning resource centres, provide essential material for supporting the curriculum, underpinning developing literacy and problem solving skills, pursuing personal interests and, of course, reading for pleasure. They support learning and teaching throughout the school and satisfy the resource requirements of both staff and students.

A library is only as good, however, as the quality of the material it contains and the ease of access it provides for its users. Efficient stock management is essential for effective resource provision and this Guideline is intended to help school library staff with the practical aspects. All types of library material will be examined, including items held in classroom book corners – typically found in the primary sector. Text books and reading scheme materials are excluded from the recommendations made here, though some of the criteria, for selection or discarding for example, might usefully be applied to this type of material as well.

The work of managing the library stock is on-going. There is never a point at which it is possible to say, 'The library is complete', only that the current phase of the work is finished. Stock management is also cyclical (see illustration below). If you are starting a new library, or developing an existing one, we would recommend that you start with creating a policy for the service your library gives within your school and then go on to development planning, because these documents help you to make decisions about all the other aspects of stock management. You would then continue with the cycle. Once a good library policy and development plan are both in place, it is possible to start anywhere in this cycle, just remember to re-evaluate the development plan at the appropriate time.

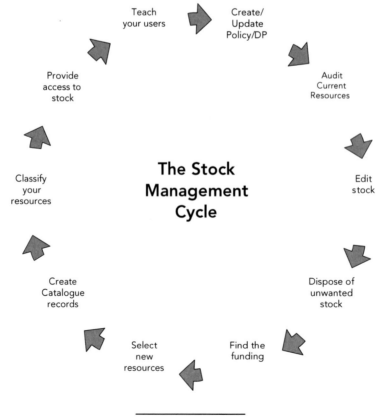

Teach your users

Create/ Update Policy/DP

Provide access to stock

Audit Current Resources

The Stock Management Cycle

Classify your resources

Edit stock

Create Catalogue records

Dispose of unwanted stock

Select new resources

Find the funding

Create a Library Policy and Development Plan

Library Policy

Every school library needs a policy statement, based on the school's development plan and self evaluation, that makes clear the role the library has in fulfilling that vision. While the librarian may write it, it is best if it is created by a group of interested staff. In a primary school the best ideas come from the staff exploring together what they need from the library, and in the secondary sector by a selected or self-selected focus group. There may already be a library committee, or one could be created for this purpose. Any such group would ideally have at least one member of the school's senior leadership team (SLT) and preferably a governor and possibly some student representatives.

The main purposes of a Library Policy are to:

- make the role of the library within the school clear to staff, governors, parents, inspectors and others
- provide a starting point for evaluating the service provided
- support budget bids for resourcing and staffing the library
- help inform development planning.

The Library Policy can address issues such as accommodation, library access, selection and discarding of stock, services provided to students and teaching staff, and staffing of the library. It is a statement of what the library should be doing, and provides a basis on which to assess the current situation. For more details about developing a Library Policy, see the SLA Guidelines: *Paperwork Made Easy: Policy Making and Development Planning for the Secondary School Library* by Lynn Winkworth and Geoff Dubber and *Practical Paperwork: Policy Making and Development Planning for the Primary School Library* by Kay Harrison and Tricia Adams.

Library Development Plan

The Library Policy should highlight the areas where the library can contribute to the development of the school and the pupils. It can identify areas where the library needs to develop its practices or resources and these can form the basis of a Library Development Plan (LDP) which in turn should become part of the School Improvement Plan (SIP). This too needs to be widely circulated and agreed by all the primary school staff; or submitted by a development/focus group to the head teacher and SMT in a middle or secondary school.

'A policy in fact is a working document. It is a summary of the school's current library practices and a series of statements about how the school wants it to be used. In some cases the library policy document may well include practices that are assumed to be understood by one and all but have never been formulated on paper.'

— Practical Paperwork: Policy Making and Development Planning for the Primary School Library by Kay Harrison and Tricia Adams

Content

The Library Development Plan needs to note the current provision, short and long term targets and objectives to fulfil the requirements of the Library Policy, and put into place methods of evaluating the level of success achieved. These will be specific to the needs of each school and created to meet particular requirements or gaps in provision. Examples of specific aims might be:

- to increase the fiction borrowing of 13-year-old boys
- to improve the science stock
- to introduce an Acceptable Use Internet Policy
- to create an out-of-hours Study Support Centre or Homework Club.

Before the LDP is written take a good look at the current provision of books and other material, including access to digital resources, in order to assess what improvement is needed (see next section).

Resources to help you with this include the SLA Guidelines: *Paperwork Made Easy: Policy Making and Development Planning for the Secondary School Library* by Lynn Winkworth and Geoff Dubber and *Practical Paperwork: Policy Making and Development Planning for the Primary School Library* by Kay Harrison and Tricia Adams. SLA members can also access and download examples of Policies and Development Plans – look for the *Paperwork Made Easy* supplementary materials at http://www.sla.org.uk/online-publications.

Audit Current Resources

The next step in the stock management cycle is to carry out an audit of current resources. This is important because it will give you an idea of the number of resources so you can see if you need to increase them to achieve the minimum recommendation of 10 items per pupil. (See SLA *Standards for Secondary School Libraries,* p6, available at www.sla.org.uk/standards). This 10 book ratio also applies to primary school libraries. If you also include a qualitative check of the resources in your audit (see section entitled Quick Book Estimate) you will also know whether the resources have current information, are attractive to staff and pupils and are relevant to the school's curriculum.

Quick Book Estimate

A good way of getting a quick estimate of current provision (especially if you have a very large library) is to sample the book stock. To do this you can look at every tenth book in each classification section, until you have a sufficient number to give you a reasonable statistical sample. In a small section like the 100s, you may need to sample the whole collection; but in larger sections look at every tenth book until you have seen around fifty. For sections which are split into two or more subject areas, sample each subject. So for the 900s you would sample both the history and geography sections up to around fifty books in each. Do the same for the fiction collection, by sampling each alphabetical section until you have about twenty books from each. If your fiction collection is separated into different sequences for different age groups, then sample each of these.

For each book that you look at note whether it is:

- less than two years old in that edition
- between two and ten years old
- older than ten years
- attractive and in good condition or battered and looking old-fashioned.

If you have date labels inside the books you can also check whether it has been borrowed in:

- the last year
- the last five years
- the last ten years
- never, or not in the last ten years.

E-Resources

E-resources should be counted in the overall provision of the library. Although they will not deteriorate physically, it is important to regularly assess them for their continued relevance to the curriculum and the school's age range.

E-resources for non-fiction are often expensive so it is essential that they are used by both staff and pupils. You can ascertain their use by asking relevant staff how often they make use of them in lessons and how often students use them for homework assignments.

Fiction e-books are not going to date in the same way as physical resources and their content does not date in the way that non fiction e-resources will, so there is less pressure to regularly assess and weed them, especially if you are subscribing to one of the e-book platforms supplied by library suppliers (see Appendix 4 for a list of suppliers).

Other Collections

Any non-book materials such as files of cuttings, maps, posters, videos, DVDs and audiobooks need to be assessed, but as there are usually far fewer of these, it is feasible to assess each item individually.

Do remember to assess any books held in classrooms for project work. Ideally, in secondary schools, material held in any satellite libraries belonging to departments should be assessed also. This is always a matter for tactful negotiation and in some schools it may not be possible.

Once this information has been gathered, it is easy to extrapolate the percentage of stock which needs replacing, especially if the sample taken is a true reflection of the whole collection.

At the same time it is important to make a count of the number of books and other resources there are in each non-fiction subject area, to ensure that the library stock supports the whole curriculum and not just some areas of it. A total for fiction books (but not reading scheme material) should also be calculated. Include any fiction held in classroom book corners, but sets of books used as class readers should not be included in this figure, as they are not available for individual use (except for the classes studying these texts).

Any items on long-term loan from your local Schools Library Service (SLS) should be included in the sampling process and calculations of stock levels, as they are an integral part of your library resource provision. See Appendix 2 for an example of a data collection sheet for a stock audit.

At this point it is usually possible to get a clear idea of how much work needs to be done, the number of new resources needed and how much it will cost to bring the library's resources up to the level required to actively achieve the statements outlined in the Library Policy and the Development Plan.

Recommendations

The School Library Association recommends that the average number of items held should be a minimum of 10 per pupil, in both primary and secondary schools; 15 would be a reasonable number to aim for. The maximum number usually required would be around 20 per pupil, but these figures need to be adjusted for the size of school. So the smallest rural primary school should be resourced as if it had no less than 200 children, to allow each of them access to a good range of materials to suit their needs, interests and abilities: 200 x 15 books = 3000. A large secondary school will enjoy economies of scale, so the maximum stock required to meet all its students' needs effectively will be about 17,000 items. Any school with a sixth form will need to increase the provision for these students owing to the wide range of subjects taught; a sixth-form college may find that the requirement is more like 20 to 25 items per student.

The SLA suggests in its *Standards for Secondary School Libraries* that the proportion of fiction to non-fiction should be around 50:50. However, as more and more information is provided electronically these proportions are likely to change in favour of fiction.

Of course, a large stock does not necessarily equate with quality stock. All these items need to be up to date and attractive, with current information and appropriate access points (contents list, index, glossary). So a certain amount of stock editing will need to take place on a regular basis to weed out inappropriate and out-of-date material.

Edit the Stock

The purpose of stock editing, or 'weeding', is to remove the material that is no longer required, or suitable, for the stock of the school library. The only way to do this thoroughly is to examine each book or other item individually, to decide whether it should remain or not. If this has not been done for some time editing could remove large numbers of books from the shelves. This can be a little disturbing, and may need to be justified to other staff/colleagues within the school. However, if the process is carried out in order to fulfil the purposes of the Library Policy and Development Plan, it can be demonstrated that this is a positive, planned activity, which will ultimately benefit the pupils and staff. It is also demonstrably true that the 'leaner and fitter' library not only looks more attractive and visually welcoming but is of more use to the pupils than one which is padded out with irrelevant, out-of-date and unappealing stock. You can always use the gaps on the shelves to display good items face on – this always improves the look of the library shelves and generates renewed interest in the resources.

Recommendations

The School Library Association recommends that the active life of a resource item is around ten years. Subjects such as science, technology and geography will need to be examined and possibly replaced after about five years (see SLA *Standards for Secondary School Libraries* p6). Paperback fiction also needs a close examination after five years and needs replacing as soon as the condition deteriorates. Schools usually need to make provision for discarding and replacing around ten per cent of the book stock each year, but if this has not been done for some time, there may be a larger proportion of books which need withdrawing.

Primary schools

In primary schools stock editing can be carried out in several different ways. It can be done as a whole-staff activity on an INSET day. Each member of staff goes to the library and selects two or three books or other items which they feel should be withdrawn from stock. They then explain to their colleagues why this is so and a list of criteria is developed for weeding the sections. Everyone then works on a section, sometimes in pairs, and editing according to the agreed criteria. This is a good way for teachers to familiarise themselves with the materials in the library and gain ownership.

If the school subscribes to the local Schools Library Service, it may be possible to pay for SLS staff to edit the library stock. In this case criteria should be agreed in advance so that the school knows what to expect from the work, and school library staff can also be involved. In primary schools this is particularly important as these teachers will often have closer links with their library and feel more ownership.

Alternatively, SLS staff will sometimes train up small teams of teachers, governors or teaching assistants (TAs) to use an agreed set of criteria. It is usually not a good idea to include parents in this activity as they have less knowledge of the curriculum and the range of abilities in the school. It can also be inhibiting for teaching staff to have parents observing the discarding of books which they have donated or raised funds for in the past.

Secondary schools

In a secondary school stock editing is usually the task of the school library staff, although in some schools each department sends one member of staff to assist with their subject area and an activity similar to that outlined above may then be appropriate.

Criteria

It is often the case that the criteria for weeding resources have already been established as part of the Library Policy, and so everyone involved in the process is aware of these from the beginning. The School Library Association recommends that the following points should be considered when developing such criteria:

- non-fiction books and other information material must be relevant to the curriculum or students' leisure interests, and must contain current, accessible information with appropriate access points, such as an index, a contents page and a bibliography
- fiction should contain good characterisation and storyline and enrich the reader with the quality of imagination and language used
- books must support individual private reading or research
- resources must be appropriate to the age and ability level of the whole school community
- resources need to be visually attractive to compete in the current world of the Internet, videos and DVDs
- resources should be free from bias, whether of gender, race, religion, politics or disability
- it is essential that all students are able to find books which reflect their own identity, especially in relation to culture and race. In primary schools especially, dual-language and mother-tongue material may be required, and in all schools resources reflecting the multicultural nature of today's society should be available.

Dispose of old/unwanted stock

Disposal of the unwanted items is the next task. This can sometimes be a challenge. Those that are in poor condition, or contain out-of-date or biased information, should be sealed into boxes and discarded or pulped. Second-hand book dealers will occasionally take old books that are in good condition, so it is sometimes worth asking them to take a look. Discarded fiction that is in good condition can be put into school sales or given to charity shops, as long as there is nothing offensive in the books (comments that could now be deemed racist or sexist, for example), provided they don't find their way back into school. Books to be donated to third world countries need to be assessed carefully, as much that is discarded here will not be of use anywhere else. It is often better to have a sale of suitable items and send the money instead.

Cuttings files and posters, where these are maintained, are not usually weeded for age, but only for subjects that are no longer taught, as older material is still valid to show the development of ideas or conflicts.

Other non-book material also needs to go through a regular editing process. Software becomes outdated or corrupt; video and audio resources may be damaged or the content no longer appropriate; and older technology, such as slides and filmstrips, may no longer be used in the school.

Historical items

Sometimes, if the library has not been edited for many years, interesting examples of books published in earlier decades come to light. In one LEA in the 1990s, many primary school libraries housed a book on rockets containing the phrase 'Some scientists believe that one day man will go to the moon'; while an inner city girls' school still had on its shelves books from the early years of the twentieth century with details of how to knit a vest or a bathing suit, or containing illustrations of students in gym-slips taking physical exercise by swinging clubs and marching. These are fantastic examples of the literature for children at the time and can be useful for history lessons. Such items can be the basis of a Heritage Collection. They should be clearly marked as such and not put back on the open shelves, but preserved elsewhere. Older material of local relevance may be precious and should also be preserved in a similar way. If items are particularly old or delicate it may be necessary to protect them with tissue paper and boxes made from acid-free materials.

Other collections

Classroom collections in primary schools should be included in this process, as this will ensure much more effective management and use of resources. It is a good idea to bring all book corner material to the central library in order to assess it. Each class teacher can then choose a new selection from the resources remaining, and begin an exchange system which will enable circulation of books and other resources every term or every year, as desired.

Ideally, departmental libraries in secondary schools should also be part of this stock editing process. Many heads of department will be delighted for the library staff to work on their collections. The support of the head teacher or the Senior Leadership Team (SLT) will help to ensure that these books are weeded to the same criteria as the library collections.

Find the Funding

Sufficient funding

How much money will you spend? In order that the school library can be an effective provider of fiction and information material, sufficient funding needs to be available to allow the managed development of the library. If you are planning to maintain the current level of resources you will need funding for replacement of approximately ten per cent of the stock each year (see section on stock editing). To increase the level of resources will require extra money.

The appropriate level of funding can be calculated by multiplying an average book price by the number of books to be purchased, and adding the cost of any non-book materials required, calculated in a similar way. More detail about budgeting for school libraries can be found in the relevant SLA Guidelines: *Making Ends Meet: Planning and Managing the Primary School Library Budget* and *Careful with Cash: Managing the Secondary School Library Budget.*

Average book prices can be obtained from the SLA website in the members section http://www.sla.org.uk/advice-average-price.php. Alternatively you can use the average cost of the books bought for your school library in the last year. This figure should be available from your Library Management System.

Recommendations

The School Library Association recommends that school governors and senior leadership provide sufficient funding for at least ten per cent of the library stock (including any held in classroom collections) to be replaced each year, with additional funding made available to bring the resources up to the recommended minimum levels (see page 8). Some of these resources, however, could be provided by short- and long-term loans from a Schools Library Service (SLS), a cost-effective way of increasing stock. A proportion of these loaned books can usually be exchanged regularly. Contact your local SLS for details of their full range of services. A full list of SLSs is available from the SLA website at http://www.sla.org.uk/schools-library-services-uk.php.

Select New Resources

Prioritising

When the library stock has been thoroughly edited it will now be possible to assess the gaps in resources and to begin active selection to meet the needs of the school as fully as possible. Take account of any changes in the curriculum and the leisure interests of the students before deciding what to spend funds on. If a large number of items has been weeded out, it may not be possible, or even desirable, to replace them all in the first year. Replacement over two or three years may need to be built into the Library Development Plan. Prioritising the expansion of sections of the library may also be necessary, especially if the school follows a two-year cycle in teaching some areas of the curriculum. There is little point in buying books immediately for a topic that will not be covered again until the year after next. The Library Development Plan will make the resource priorities clear.

As with editing, ideally teaching colleagues should be involved in the stock selection process. The library staff will need to consult regularly with teachers and support staff across the school to ensure that appropriate curriculum support is provided and maintained. Teachers may request purchase of specific titles which they know about through their professional reading or subject associations.

Information about new resources

Criteria for selection of new stock are likely to be similar to those adopted for editing purposes (see above). They should be already agreed and outlined in the stock selection section of the Library Policy.

There are a variety of ways of finding out about new resources. With more than 8,000 new titles for children and young people published every year in the UK alone, some shortcuts are needed to selecting the right ones. Reviewing journals, such as our own *The School Librarian*, *Carousel* and *Books for Keeps*, all provide a selection of excellent and reliable reviews (details in Appendix 5). Some children's books are reviewed occasionally in the *Times Educational Supplement* and national newspapers. *The School Librarian* also contains a regular review section for websites and e-resources.

Some school library services maintain an exhibition collection of recommended titles published in the last year or two, and may provide written reviews. Many organisations publish book lists on specific subjects relevant to their field of interest.

The SLA Riveting Reads series of publications contains lists of recommended and reviewed titles covering a wide range of subject matter and levels of difficulty. They are grouped under themes and have been recommended by pupils in the relevant age group.

Recommendations can be invited from students about the books they would like to see in the library.

A visit to the showroom of a library supplier specialising in children's books will provide a hands-on opportunity to examine the books, although there will be no pre-selection as in the methods mentioned above. It is also possible to use information from individual publishers, obtained from catalogues, websites or visits from publishers' reps, although it is important not to be swayed by special offers, but to select only what you know you need for the library.

Buying books

There are many places where school librarians and teachers can go to buy books. Library suppliers (see Appendix 4) provide large warehouse showrooms where it is possible to see a wide range of materials under one roof. These may be multiple-copy showrooms, where you take the items you want to buy and put them on a trolley. Alternatively, single-copy showrooms have only one copy of each title and you need to create a list of those you wish to order. While most of these books will be in stock, with this method it is always wise to order some extra titles as there are usually some that will be out of stock or even out of print. In both cases you will be told exactly how much you have spent at regular intervals, and after your visit you will be sent a printout of the titles selected.

Buying e-books

There are lots of suppliers of e-books available but not all of them have resources suitable for library lending. You will need to read the terms and conditions of sale before buying items as they may be for personal use only. There are currently four main suppliers of e-books for school libraries:

- Browns Books for Students have a platform called **VLebooks**

    http://www.brownsbfs.co.uk/StoreFront/Pages/VLeBooks

- MLS in conjunction with OverDrive (the American suppliers who are used by most public library authorities) offer the **Eclipse School Download Library**

    http://www.microlib.co.uk/home/eBooks.aspx.

- Peters Books and Furniture in conjunction with Wheelers (a New Zealand based company) offer **Peters ePlatform**

    http://petersbooks.co.uk/our-services/e-platform

- RM Books offer their **RM Bookshelf** rental system

    https://www.rmbookshelf.com/

Non-fiction e-resources are available from suppliers such as JCS http://jcsonlineresources.org or Gale http://gale.cengage.co.uk. They come in bundles and you buy a subscription to the resources you want.

Servicing

The advantage of buying from library suppliers is that they will do all the servicing, or preparation, of your books if you wish and deliver them ready to go on the shelves. Servicing can include covering, attaching spine labels, computer barcodes and date labels, or providing tickets to your specification. Library suppliers will also insert security tags and stamp the books with your school stamp. There is a small charge for this, but it saves large amounts of time for school library staff who can then spend more time working with students and concerning themselves with library development.

If you use one of the main computerised library management systems, they can also provide you with records in the appropriate format to download on to your system, although you will have to add any keywords required. Discounts can be negotiated, and often the more you spend at any one time the greater the discount will be.

It is also possible to arrange discounts with local bookshops. These are best used for purchases of titles that you know you wish to buy, as they can stock only a small number of titles to select from and they will rarely provide any servicing of books. On-line booksellers such as Amazon (www.amazon.co.uk), on the other hand, provide you with a vast range of information which can equally make selection difficult; and they also will not provide servicing. Some Schools Library Services have a bookshop facility linked to their exhibition collection.

Buying from publishers' reps can be a useful way of selecting small numbers of books, but keeping appointments with reps from all the major publishers can be very time-consuming and you cannot make comparisons with similar titles from other publishers. It is rarely a good idea to buy remaindered books, however cheap they are, if the information in them could date. Check the date of publication before being tempted.

Create Catalogue Records

Once you have obtained the new items you need to make a record of them. This is known as an acquisition record. Most school librarians use their computer database for this purpose. Almost all secondary schools, and an increasing number of primary schools, now use a purpose-built library management system to record their stock, provide a searchable database for student and staff access to the resources, and create records of loans. Most of these databases will automatically assign a unique identifying number, which can also be printed on a barcode attached to the item. For those schools without an ICT system, a card or paper-based record will be needed.

Cataloguing

A catalogue record of each item is necessary in order to manage the library resources effectively and make them easier to find. Each record should contain several items of essential information:

- Title
- Author
- Publisher
- Date of publication
- Dewey classification number or fiction (see next section)
- Date of purchase
- Type of media (book, video, website and so on).

In addition it is a good idea to include:

- at least one, and preferably several, suitable keywords that will help make searching for the item easier, and thus make it more accessible to both students and staff
- price
- location, if not in the main library.

Computer record

All of the major Library Management Systems have a standard catalogue screen to complete when inputting material for the first time. It is necessary only to fill in as required. Examples are shown here from three popular library management systems.

Oliver from Softlink Europe

Heritage from IS Oxford

Eclipse.net from Microlibrarian Systems

Card Catalogue

If a computer is not used, then secondary school staff may wish to consider developing, or restoring, a card catalogue. This will involve three sequences of catalogue cards:

- each non-fiction book will need an entry in all of them, while fiction books will need entries in two
- A subject index will also be required for the non-fiction; and preferably a keyword index for the fiction
- A subject index is a comprehensive listing of subjects covered by the non-fiction items in the library, and the Dewey numbers where these items have been classified (see next section). Setting up and maintaining such a catalogue is very time consuming, and schools might be better advised to spend their time setting up a computer system. If this is not possible, the card sequences required are:

    i. author entry (non-fiction and fiction titles)

    ii. title entry (non-fiction and fiction titles)

    iii. classified entry (non-fiction only).

For examples of these, and of keyword entries, see Appendix 3.

Management information

It is very difficult for the staff of a primary school to keep this type of card catalogue up to date and therefore to be really useful. But it is important to ensure that information is available for two purposes: to provide information about items bought, for management purposes; and to provide access to the material for students and staff. If a primary school does not have a computer management system, information can be provided by making lists of new stock on a word processor or simple database, and making counts of older material not already listed. To enable access to the resources, it is possible to use a printed subject index. Subject indexes are produced by some Schools Library Services for use by their local primary schools, and items on loan from them will match their index. If there is not one available locally, a Subject Index for Primary Schools is an integral part of the School Library Association's *Primary School Classification Scheme* (see page 36). This has been created to be relevant to all countries of the British Isles and is licensed by OCLC.

Wall chart

In addition to a comprehensive subject index, a simplified wall chart can be of use in primary schools to enable children to find the most popular subjects quickly, and to help them to understand the relationship between Dewey numbers and the order of books. Some primary schools create a new one each term, covering the topics they will be teaching.

For a full explanation of how to make a wallchart and an example please refer to page 12 of *Check It Out: Issue Systems for the Primary School Library* by Tricia Adams and Kathy Lemaire.

E-Resources

The modern Library Management Systems also make it possible to include e-resources in their databases. Websites, e-books and databases can all be catalogued and this will help staff and pupils use them effectively. You will need to follow the rules for cataloguing for your particular system.

Classify your Resources

Dewey System

In order to make it possible to find items when they are required, it is necessary to arrange them in a logical order. In most school libraries they will be organised in a numerical system called the Dewey Decimal Classification scheme (DDC). This is also used in the majority of UK public and university libraries, so a pupil who has learned to use the scheme in school will be able to transfer this skill to other libraries. DDC has been in use for well over a hundred years and has been revised regularly to take account of new branches of knowledge and new subjects that need to be classified.

All knowledge is divided up into ten classes, which are numbered from 000 to 900. Each class is then broken down individually to provide more specific numbers from 001 to 999. Finally decimal places are used to add further distinction within subjects.

It is usual for schools to use a truncated version of DDC as some of the numbers can be very long. Classifying with numbers of up to two decimal places is suitable for middle and secondary schools, and in primary schools it should not be necessary to use numbers after the decimal point in more than a few cases; for history books, for example, where it is necessary to separate different chronological periods for the same country. Infant schools will not usually need any decimal places at all.

The School Library Association publishes a primary version of the DDC suitable for use in Scotland, Wales, Ireland and England. This also provides instructions on how to classify books. The full Dewey scheme and the abridged version are available from OCLC (http://www.oclc.org/en-UK/home.html). The abridged version of Dewey is suitable for secondary schools (http://www.oclc.org/en-UK/dewey/versions/abridged.html).

Colour coding

Some primary schools may elect to use a colour coding system to help children locate books easily. It is not possible to use colour coding to organise a whole collection of non-fiction effectively because there are only a small range of colours available. If a colour coding scheme is used, it is best used in conjunction with a simplified Dewey scheme, to aid pupils in finding the general sections. Experience shows that children, even at infant level, can handle the Dewey system in a simple form, and that it will help reinforce numeracy skills.

Provide Easy Access

Shelving

The majority of library resources are books, which require appropriate shelving to contain and protect them and make them available to students and staff. Books are shelved from left to right and down each bay of shelves, before starting at the top of the next bay. They are also normally shelved in a logical sequence around the room in order of class number or Dewey number for non-fiction and alphabetical order of author's name for fiction. A separate section for reference-only material can also be set up. It makes sense to follow these conventions. This is the way in which most other libraries shelve their books so will be a real advantage for pupils to learn and understand this sequence, especially for those who go on to further or higher education.

As books are not all the same size, and as you may wish to move sections of the stock to new locations, it is important that the shelving is adjustable. It is also essential to ensure that the shelving you choose has integral bookstops or supports as part of the system, to avoid books falling over and sliding off the shelf. This type of shelving is usually made of metal, and comes in a variety of colours. It can also have end panels attached if required, for posters or general display. Shelving systems of this nature will allow for interchangeable display shelves and storage facilities for runs of journals or magazines to be incorporated. Shelves of different widths are available for fiction and non-fiction books. Picture books are best kept in kinderboxes - low wooden boxes on legs with divisions to allow several runs of picture books to be contained, front cover out. These books are not normally stored in any order, but with a large collection it can be useful to have each kinderbox dedicated to a section of the alphabet and house the books according to the first letter of the authors' surname.

Recommendations

It is important not to have shelving that is too high, so that the youngest pupil in the school can reach the top shelves without too much trouble. The usual recommendation is a maximum height of:

- 1200 mm for primary schools
- 1500 mm for middle schools
- 1800 mm for secondary schools.

It is also better not to have the bottom shelves too low as resources on these shelves can be overlooked. Schools with students who have physical difficulties will have no problems adjusting their shelves to suit their users providing they have bought adjustable shelving.

Labels indicating where particular subjects are kept – called guiding – should be attached to the shelves. As the stock may be moved around the shelves, depending on curriculum need and what is on loan, it is important that the guiding is not fixed. A slot at the front of the shelving is ideal for this purpose.

Health and safety

Safety is an important factor in deciding which shelves to use. A bay of shelving full of books is very heavy, so DIY shelving is rarely adequate and is often dangerous. Buy shelving which has been designed for the purpose, and ensure it is fixed to the wall if this is what is intended by the manufacturer.

See Appendix 4 for a list of suppliers.

Non-book material

Storage for non-book material is usually available from shelving suppliers, and can range from expensive cabinets to vinyl wallets suspended from metal holders. Make sure that it is possible to label items adequately, and display them for selection when required.

E-readers will need to be kept in a secure cupboard or cabinet but will also need facilities for recharging.

Laptops will also need secure storage. Special trolleys can be purchased with inbuilt recharging facilities and these will make it easier to issue and return the laptops.

See Appendix 4 for a list of suppliers.

Security

A well-equipped school library is a very valuable resource. The replacement cost for all the items in it will be many thousands of pounds. Although loss from fire, flood or other disaster cannot be avoided, it is possible to minimise losses due to absent minded pupils and staff and the rare deliberate theft.

Minimising losses

There are many ways of achieving this. Computers, e-readers and other hardware can be indelibly marked and physically constrained. The items that 'walk' most regularly, however, are books. Many schools now minimise these losses by using specialist library security systems, and occasionally by installing video surveillance equipment, if it is in use elsewhere in the school.

Library security systems rely on a tag inserted in the book in a place where it is difficult for potential thieves to find it – usually down the spine, under the barcode label, or between two pages close to the spine of the book. These tags are initially inserted in the existing stock, but if new books are serviced by a library supplier they will insert tags for you. Some people only insert tags in expensive books, but it is probably better to use the system in every book if it is in use at all. The main cost in such systems is in the security gates, so to tag only a portion of the stock is a false economy. It is probably unwise to allow students, however trustworthy, to assist with this procedure, as the location of the tags could become common knowledge within the school and pupils may try to remove them.

The tags are activated so that they will sound an alarm when passed through security gates. Some systems rely on the tags being de-activated when the item is loaned, while others remain activated and the items are passed around the security gate by staff. The latter system can pose a problem for students, however, as these items occasionally trigger alarms in shops or in the public library.

Schools which have invested in a security system have shown that such a system, while expensive initially, can dramatically reduce losses and pay for itself in a relatively short time, assuming the library is constantly staffed. A general rule of thumb is that if the cost of installing a system is less than the value of items lost over five years, it is worth installing. The value of missing books can be estimated during the annual stock check (see page 24).

Modern security systems can also include Radio Frequency Identification (RFID) issuing whereby pupils can issue and return their own books. Although an expensive system to install this would make sense in a library that is not staffed for part of the day or evening.

Primary schools

Most primary schools are unlikely to find a security system of benefit, as their libraries are rarely staffed continuously, and in any case they are less likely to have a serious problem with losses.

For details of suppliers of some of these systems, see Appendix 4.

Teach your Library Users

Once the library is ready, it is important that staff and students are taught how to use it. If major changes have been made, the whole school community would benefit from learning how an issue system works, for example, or how to use the new catalogue. Guided tours and printed handouts will help, but each class will need its first session in the revamped or new library to be one of exploration and discovery. If only minor changes have taken place, they can be incorporated into an on-going information skills programme. New students and staff will need induction sessions in the library.

The SLA Guidelines series includes titles giving advice on library induction and on developing information skills. For primary schools there is *Cultivating Curiosity: Information Literacy Skills and the Primary School Library* by Geoff Dubber and its accompanying publication A Primary School Information Skills Toolkit by Geoff Dubber. For secondary schools check out *Plans, Practices and Policies: Information Literacy and the Secondary School Library* by Geoff Dubber.

There are also lesson plans and ideas for activities around induction and the teaching of library skills on the SLA website www.sla.org.uk/learning-and-teaching. These are free for SLA members to download and use.

Grand opening

It is often a good exercise in raising the library profile to have a grand opening of a new or revamped library. This can be the highlight of a book week, with visiting authors and storytellers. Some schools take the opportunity of making a video, showing the before and after scenes, as well as what happened in between. At this point it is important to stop and catch your breath and give yourself a pat on the back for what you have achieved. Well-earned praise can be given to all those who have helped, before the whole stock management cycle begins again.

The Annual Stock Check
(the process begins again)

Once a catalogue has been set up in the school library, it is useful to carry out an annual or perhaps biennial stock check. This may require the library to be closed for about a week, and so in a secondary school it is usually undertaken out of school time. In many school libraries the time chosen is at the end of the summer term, either before or after the school has broken up.

Participants on the School Librarian Network in July 2013 commented:

"I always do my fiction stock take in February and the non-fiction May/June when Year 11,12 & 13 are on study leave. I don't close the library – I really don't think this is necessary. Your LMS should be able to set up a stock take (we use Heritage), and you just need to make sure that you pass anything that has come back from being on loan through it. I find it is particularly useful for weeding non-fiction and sorting out anomalies."

"I do an annual stocktake in the penultimate week of the summer term, closing the library to do so. I find it very useful to keep the catalogue accurate for students and a way of fitting in essential stock work, such as weeding and identifying stock needs, at the same time! I flag it up to staff and students well in advance (it's in the school calendar) and allow double borrowing the week before and after so borrowers don't miss out. It's accepted by school as a regular event and doesn't affect our loans adversely. All schools are different though, so I hope you can find a way that suits both you and your school from all the different suggestions offered in this thread. Good luck!"

It might be possible to arrange for the local Schools Library Service to carry out the annual stock check.

Missing items

As well as assessing the library resources for condition and use, each item is checked against its catalogue record, to identify those items that are missing. Many computerised library management systems make this a relatively easy activity to carry out, and it can often be done with a hand-held data capture unit. With a manual catalogue, it is necessary to check each resource against it, and any items not found must be checked against the record of those out on loan before marking them as missing. The catalogue cards for any lost items should then be removed from every sequence. In a secondary school, if there are serious losses, it may be necessary to consider installing a security system.

It is always a good idea, however, to declare an 'amnesty' in school before carrying out a stock check. Dump bins can be placed around the school so that students can anonymously return items that are long overdue or where the loan was never recorded. The loss of any small fines in such instances is normally more than offset by the value of the returned items.

Overdue loans

During the school year, reminders of overdue items should be sent out on a regular basis, and while the first one is usually to the pupil (except in the case of the youngest children), the second reminder is often addressed to the class teacher or form tutor. Many schools send final overdue notices, including the cost of the item, to the parents. Withdrawal of library privileges is occasionally used as a final sanction for persistent offenders, although many schools believe that this is not the right solution. Similarly, many secondary schools do not charge fines for overdue books, as this may disadvantage some children and make them less likely to return items. Primary schools almost never charge fines. Secondary schools may also request a deposit before issuing e-readers or laptops so that the cost of repairing any damage can be deducted from the deposit before returning it at the end of term.

If a primary school has lists of only the more recent books, then only these can be stock checked. However, it is still possible to monitor any issue system to ensure books are returned, and to make a count of library items to make sure that the school is not losing valuable resources in large quantities.

Resources on loan from a Schools Library Service should be included in any stock check.

Appendix 1:
Care and Repair of Books

An attractive, clean and cared-for book is much more likely to encourage children to pick it up and to take care of it themselves. It is always worthwhile putting some time and effort into this. Volunteer parents and students can be used for this chore, as it gives a feeling of pride and ownership to transform a book and return it to circulation.

When returned books are being put back on the shelves, they should always be quickly assessed for condition. Any that are vandalised, badly damaged or falling apart need to be disposed of, but not before a note has been made of the title and author so that a replacement can be bought. A newer edition, or even an alternative title, may need to be purchased. Fiction can often be bought with a more modern cover, and increasingly hardback fiction is giving way to paperback, which students prefer both to read and to carry.

The record of a discarded item will need to be removed from any catalogue, whether manual (such as card catalogue), or computerised.

Books that are not badly damaged, or are dirty, can be repaired or cleaned and put back into circulation.

Plastic jackets

Plastic jackets are used to cover and protect paper jackets on hardback books and the card covers on paperbacks. They should be cleaned, if looking a little grubby, with a cloth dampened with a weak solution of washing-up liquid. Some marks may require white spirit, and there is now a patent book cleaning fluid which you may wish to use. Be careful to store these fluids safely and out of the reach of children. Make sure that the books are dry before they are put back on the shelf, as otherwise they will stick together and they may become smelly.

Damaged or worn plastic jackets should be replaced with new ones. Be careful how you attach these to the book, so that they do not tear an attractive endpaper when they are replaced. Spine labels should also be replaced. Be careful to ensure that they are covered with a badge protector or Scotch 'Magic Tape'. It is important not to use ordinary transparent tape as this will go yellow and fall off, leaving a nasty residue.

Pages

Books that have pages missing should be disposed of, as they will be of no use to students.

If the pages are not too badly torn it is possible to repair them with Scotch 'Magic Tape'. This matt tape, while looking opaque on the roll, will disappear on the page and is much more suitable for repair of pages than other types of shiny sticky tape. If there are a lot of damaged pages in a book, it is better to replace it.

Grubby pages can sometimes be transformed by cleaning them with a clean white eraser, while a small indelible scribble can be Tippexed out.

Covers

If the covers have come away from a hardback book, and the rest of the book is still up to date and in good condition, it is possible to stick them back, but it is not an easy job to make the book look good.

1. First coat the exposed bound spine with a strong paper adhesive.

2. Lay the book in the correct position with the outer cover facing down and tape the front cover to the front endpaper with a strong, sticky-backed linen tape.

3. Turn the book to the back and tape this cover in place also, ensuring that you keep the spine against the cover, so that the adhesive will hold.

4. Finally, close the book and bind tightly with strong elastic bands or string, to ensure that it remains in this position until the adhesive has dried (for a few days will be best).

It is always a good idea, particularly with primary children, to spend some time teaching them to value and take care of books. Points to be mentioned include:

- always wash hands before using a book

- never leave it on the floor to be trodden on

- never use foreign objects as bookmarks

- always close the book and return it to the shelf or kinderbox when finished with it

- never allow babies to chew books.

Adult role models are particularly important in encouraging this sort of behaviour.

Appendix 2:

Data Collection Sheet for a superficial stock audit in a school library

Use for sampling all class sections and alphabetical sections of fiction books.
Fill in using 'five bar gates'.

Dewey No. or Fiction Letter	Number looked at	Number shabby	Older than 10 years	2 to 10 years old	Newer than 2 years	Borrowed in last 2 years	Never borrowed

Appendix 3:
Simplified Library Catalogue Cards for the School Library

1: **author entry card**, to be filed in alphabetical order of author's last name (non-fiction and fiction examples shown)

HENEGHAN, JUDITH   636
Love your hamster
Wayland, 2013

COLFER, EOIN   FIC
The reluctant assassin
Puffin, 2013

2: **title entry card**, to be filed in alphabetical order of first word of title, ignoring words like 'the' and 'a' (non-fiction and fiction examples shown)

LOVE YOUR HAMSTER   636
Heneghan, Judith
Wayland, 2013

THE RELUCTANT ASSASSIN   FIC
Colfer, Eoin
Puffin, 2013

3: **subject entry card**, to be filed in numerical order (non-fiction only)

PETS   636
HENEGHAN, JUDITH
Love your hamster
Wayland, 2013

4: **keyword entry card**, to be filed alphabetically by subject (optional – fiction only)

FANTASY   FIC
COLFER, EOIN
The reluctant assassin
Puffin, 2013

Appendix 4: Library Suppliers

Books and other resources

Askews Library Services
218 – 222 North Road
Preston
PR1 1SY
Tel: 01772 555947
Email: enquiries@askews.co.uk
Web: http://www.askews.co.uk/

Bertram Library Services
Elmfield Road
Morley
Leeds
LS27 0NN
Tel: 0871 803 6900
Email: library.enquiries@bertrams.com
Web: http://www.bertrams.com/

Browns Books for Students Ltd
22 – 28 George Street
Hull
HU1 3AP
Tel: 01482325413
Email: schools.services@brownsbfs.co.uk
Web: http://www.bfs.co.uk/

Carel Press
4 Hewson Street
Carlisle
CA2 5AU
Tel: 01228 538928
Email: info@carelpress.co.uk
Web: http://www.carelpress.com/

Heath Educational Books
Willow House, Willow Walk
Sutton
Surrey SM3 9QQ
Tel: 020 8644 7788
Web: http://www.heathbooks.co.uk/

Kent Book Company
109 Hall Road
Aylesford
Kent
ME20 7RE
Tel: 01622 717827
Email: enquiries@kbc.eu.com
Web: http://www.kbc.eu.com/

Lambrick Enterprises
The Station House
Great Wacton Lane, Rowden
Bredenbury
Herefordshire
HR7 4TG
United Kingdom
Tel: 01885 489003
Email: lambrick.enterprises@virgin.net

Peters Books and Furniture
120 Bromsgrove Street
Birmingham
B5 6RL
Tel: 0121 666 6646
Email: sales@peters-books.co.uk
Web: http://www.peters-books.co.uk/

Turner Books
193-195 Chipstead Valley Road
Coulsdon
Surrey
CR5 3BR
Tel: 01737 556311
Email: info@turnerbooks.co.uk
Web: http://turnerbooks.tbpcontrol.co.uk/

E-book suppliers

Browns Books for Students
   VLebooks
22 – 28 George Street
Hull
HU1 3AP
Tel: 01482325413
http://www.brownsbfs.co.uk/StoreFront/
Pages/VLeBooks

Peters Books and Furniture
   Peters ePlatform
120 Bromsgrove Street
Birmingham
B5 6RL
Tel: 0121 666 6646
http://petersbooks.co.uk/our-services/
e-platform/

Micro Librarian Systems
   Eclipse School Download Library
Arden House. Shepley Lane
Marple, Stockport
SK6 7JW
Tel: 0161 449 9357
http://www.microlib.co.uk/home/eBooks.aspx

RM Books
   RM Bookshelf
140 Eastern Avenue, Milton Park
Abingdon
OX14 4SB
Tel: 08450 700300
https://www.rmbookshelf.com/

Examples of storage trolleys/cabinets for laptops

A. J. Products (UK) Ltd
Unit 19-20 Nimbus
Hercules Way
Farnborough
GU14 6UU
Tel: 01252 359760
Email: info@ajproducts.co.uk
Web: http://www.ajproducts.co.uk

LapSafe Products
Unit 3 Wakes Hall Business Centre
Wakes Colne
Colchester
CO6 2DY
Tel: 0800 130 3456
Email: sales@lapsafe.com
Web: http://www.lapsafe.com/

Security systems

2 CQR
Triangle Business Park
Main Street
Long Bennington
Lincolnshire
NG23 5JR
Tel: 01400 283 850

3M Library Systems
3M Centre
Cain Road
Bracknell
RG12 8HT
Tel: 08705 360036

MLS Intellident
Intellident Ltd
Landmark House
Station Road
Cheadle Hulme
Stockport
SK8 7BS
Tel: 0161 498 1140
Email: info@intellident.co.uk

Library stationery, shelving and equipment

Demco Worldwide Ltd
Demco Interiors
Shipton Way, Express Park
Rushden
Northamptonshire
NN10 6GL
Tel: 01992 454600
Email: enquiries@demcointeriors.co.uk
Web: http://www.demcointeriors.co.uk/
Demco Interiors are one of the UK's leading
library design consultancy, specialising in the
design, specification, installation and project
management of library refurbishment and new
build projects.

DPC
Britannia Storage Systems Ltd
Unit 3, Meadow Barn
Great Tay Business Centre
Warrens Farm
Great Tay
Colchester
CO6 1JG
Tel: 0845 6520049
Web: http://www.britannia-storage.co.uk/
DPC have been manufacturing and designing
library furniture for over 20 years.

FG Library Products
Concept House
Upton Valley Way East
Pineham Business Park
Northampton
NN4 9EF
Tel: 01604 755 954
Email: library@fggroup.co.uk
Web: www.fglibrary.co.uk/
FG Library Products is a design led
manufacturer of custom made library and
general office furniture. Their website provides
useful case studies of school library
refurbishments.

Finnmade Furniture Solutions Ltd.
6 Newlands Lane
Hitchin
SG4 9AY
Hertfordshire
Tel: 01462 452001
Web: http://www.finnmade.co.uk/
Finnmade Furniture Solutions specialise in the
supply and installation of shelving, furniture
and accessories for school, public and business
libraries.

Gresswell
Freepost ANG0802
Hoddesdon
Herts
EN11 0BR
Tel: 01992 45 45 11
Email: orders@gresswell.com
Web: http://www.gresswell.co.uk/
Gresswells offer a wide choice in library
supplies, furniture and display to assist you in
the smooth running of your library and to help
make your library environment an attractive
and welcoming place for visitors.

ISIS
Isis Concepts Ltd
57 High St.
Tetsworth
Oxfordshire
OX9 7BS
Tel: 01844 280 123
Web: www.isisconcepts.co.uk

Librex Educational Ltd
Colwick Road
Nottingham
NG2 4BG
Tel: 0115 950 4664/0115 958 0032
Email:sales@librex.co.uk
Web: http://www.librex.co.uk/
Librex have been an established library
supplier for almost 40 years. A comprehensive
selection of goods is offered including: Library
furniture; Charging equipment; Display
equipment.

LS Associates
Library Support Services Ltd
46 Meadowcroft Road
London
N13 4EA
Tel: 020 8351 0152
Email: info@edulib.co.uk
Website: http://www.edulib.co.uk
LS Associates supplies the widest range of
shelving and furniture systems designed
specifically for use in all types of libraries.

Opening the Book
Opening the Book Furniture Ltd
7b St Michael's Court
Warstone Parade East
Jewellery Quarter
Birmingham
B18 6NR
Tel: 0121 246 2777
Email: sales@openingthebook.com
Web: http://www.openingthebook.com/
Opening the Book have designed and
installed more than 50 libraries of all sizes and
types. Their website also has some very
useful photographic examples of libraries they
have designed, including primary
and secondary school libraries.

Peters Bookselling Services
The Kit Shop
120 Bromsgrove St,
Birmingham, B5 6RJ
Tel: 0121 666 6646
Email: sales@peters-books.co.uk
Web: http://www.peters-books.co.uk/
Peters are the largest independent library
supplier in the country. They have a new
showroom featuring all of the products
from their current range of library furniture
including shelving, display units and a
colourful selection of rugs.

Ryco Book Protection Svs Ltd
Unit 10 Ballywaltrim Business Center
Bray
Co. Wicklow
Ireland
Tel: 00353 (0) 1 2867055
Freephone in the UK: 0800 783 5156
Ryco offer a range of high quality, library
standard book covering materials and supply
to many libraries.

Serota Library Furniture
SEROTA Ltd
92 Hilliard Road
Northwood
Middlesex
HA6 1SW
Tel: 01923 840697
Email: info@serota.co.uk
Web: http://www.serota.co.uk/
The Serota family has over 100 years'
experience of furniture manufacturing and
fitting. All the furniture is custom-made so you
choose a solution that suits your space.

Library Management Systems

Access-IT Software – for primary and secondary school libraries and special schools
The Nova Building
Herschel Street
Slough SL1 1XS
Tel: 01753 701789
Email: support@accessitlibrary.co.uk
Web: http://www.accessitsoftware.com/

Alice Junior – for primary school libraries and special schools
Softlink Europe Ltd
Oak Court
North Leigh Business Park
North Leigh
Oxon OX29 6SW
Tel: 01993 883401
Email: sales@softlink.co.uk
Web: http://www.softlink.co.uk

Amlib – for secondary schools
Unit 3, 1st Floor, Parkview Business Park
Crockford Lane
Basingstoke
Hampshire RG24 8NA
Tel: 01256 300 790
Email: sales@amlib.co.uk
Websites: www.amlib.co.uk

Autolib – for secondary schools
19 Angelvale Business Park
Top Angel
Buckingham MK18 1TH
Tel: 01280 820 080
Email: sales@autolib.co.uk
Web: http://www.autolib.co.uk

Eclipse – for secondary schools
Micro Librarian Systems
Arden House
Shepley Lane
Marple
Stockport SK6 7JW
Tel: 0161 449 9357
Email: aobrien@microlib.co.uk
Web: http://www.microlib.co.uk

Heritage – for secondary schools
IS Oxford
The Chapel
3 Armstrong Road
Littlemore
Oxon OX4 4XT
Tel: 01865 481000
Email: sales@isoxford.com
Web: http://www.isoxford.com

Junior Librarian – for primary schools
Micro Librarian Systems
Arden House
Shepley Lane
Marple
Stockport SK6 7JW
Tel: 0161 449 9357
Email: aobrien@microlib.co.uk
Web: http://www.microlib.co.uk

Oliver – for secondary schools
Softlink Europe Ltd
Oak Court
North Leigh Business Park
North Leigh
Oxon OX29 6SW
Tel: 01993 883401
Fax: 01993 883799
Email: sales@softlink.co.uk
Web: http://www.softlink.co.uk

247lib.com
Applied Network Solutions Limited
The Innovation Centre
Norden House
Basing View
Basingstoke
Hampshire
RG21 4HG
Tel: 01256 300790
Email: support@answeb.co.uk
Web: http://www.247lib.com/

Appendix 5: Other Sources of Information

Journals with book reviews

Books for Keeps

http://booksforkeeps.co.uk/

Online bi-monthly magazine that should be in every primary school library; full of articles, author information, news about books, and book reviews.

Carousel

http://www.carouselguide.co.uk/

Carousel is packed with reviews, stories and articles about the world of children's books written by experts. Published three times a year.

The School Librarian

http://www.sla.org.uk/the-school-librarian

Published by the School Library Association, membership of the SLA includes a subscription to *The School Librarian* which is packed with interesting articles and age-ranged reviews of books as well as ICT and websites.

Organisations

Booktrust

Book House
45 East Hill
London
SW18 2QZ
Tel: 020 8516 2977
Web: www.booktrust.org.uk/
Charity promoting a love of books and reading.

Children's Books Ireland

Children's Books Ireland
17 North Great George's Street
Dublin 1
Tel: +353 (0)1 8727475
Web: www.childrensbooksireland.ie/
Engages young people with books, fosters a greater understanding of the importance of books and acts as a core resource for children in Ireland.

National Literacy Trust

68 South Lambeth Road
London
SW8 1RL
Tel: 020 7587 1842
Web: www.literacytrust.org.uk/
National charity dedicated to raising literacy levels in the UK.

Scottish Book Trust

Sandeman House, Trunk's Close
55 High Street
Edinburgh
EH1 1SR
Tel: 0131 524 0160
Web: www.scottishbooktrust.com
Works with people throughout Scotland to promote the pleasures and benefits of reading and books.

The Reading Agency

Free Word Centre
60 Farringdon Road
London
EC1R 3GA
Tel: 0207 324 2544
Web: http://readingagency.org.uk/
Programmes to help people feel inspired and confident about reading.

Welsh Books Council

Castell Brychan
Aberystwyth
Ceredigion
SY23 2JB
Tel: 01970 624151
Web: http://www.cllc.org.uk/
Promotes reading and literacy in Wales.

SLA Publications

Careful With Cash: Managing the Secondary School Library Budget
by Geoff Dubber and Sally Dring
2012   978-1-903446-68-3

Quality and Impact: Evaluating the Performance of your School Library
by Elspeth Scott, Sally Duncan and Geoff Dubber
2011   978-1-903446-59-1

Check It Out: Issue Systems for the Primary School Library
by Tricia Adams and Kathy Lemaire
2011   978-1-903446-56-0

Paperwork Made Easy: Policy Making and Development Planning for the Secondary School Library
by Lynn Winkworth and Geoff Dubber
2008   978-1-903446-47-8

A Primary School Information Skills Toolkit
by Geoff Dubber
2008   978-1-903446-44-7

Cultivating Curiosity: Information Literacy Skills and the Primary School Library
by Geoff Dubber
2008   978-1-903446-42-3

Practical Paperwork: Policy Making and Development Planning for the Primary School Library
by Kay Harrison and Tricia Adams
2007   978-1-903446-37-9

Primary School Classification Scheme
Pack containing A Practical Guide, Subject Index, Poster and CD-ROM
ISBN 978-1-903446-19-5